THE ULTIMATE
NEW YORK KNICKS
TRIVIA BOOK

A Collection of Amazing Trivia Quizzes
and Fun Facts for Die-Hard Knicks Fans!

Ray Walker

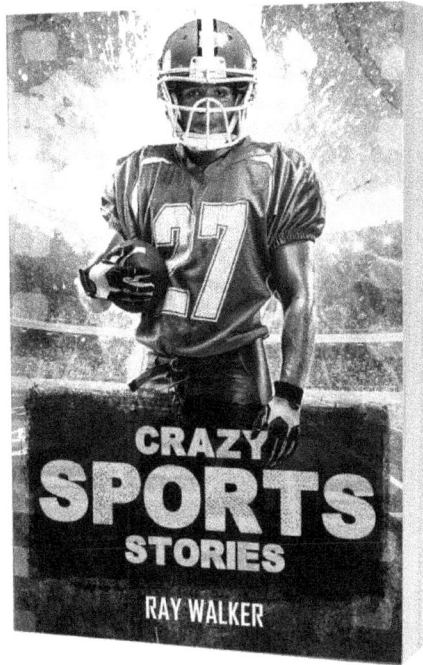

CONTENTS

INTRODUCTION

Team fandom should be inspirational. Our attachment to our favorite teams should fill us with pride, excitement, loyalty, and a sense of fulfillment in knowing that we are part of a community with many other fans who feel the same way.

New York Knicks fans are no exception. With a rich, successful history in the NBA, the Knicks have inspired their supporters to strive for greatness with their tradition of colorful players, memorable eras, big moves, and unique moments.

You may use the book as you wish, as it is meant to be a celebration of those moments, and an examination of the collection of interesting details that allow us to understand the full stories behind the players, and the team.

Each chapter contains 20 quiz questions in a mixture of multiple-choice and true or false formats, with an answer key (don't worry, it's on a separate page!), and a section of 10 "Did You Know" factoids about the team.

Some readers will use the book to test themselves with the quiz questions. How much Knicks history did you really know? How many of the finer points can you remember?

Some will use it competitively, isn't that the heart of sports, waging contests with friends and fellow devotees to see who can lay claim to being the biggest fan?

Some will enjoy it as a learning experience, gaining insight to enrich their fandom and add color to their understanding of their favorite team.

Still others may use it to teach, sharing the wonderful anecdotes inside to inspire a new generation of fans to hop aboard the Knicks bandwagon. Whatever your purpose may be, we hope you enjoy delving into the amazing background of New York Knicks basketball!

Oh, and for the record, information and statistics in this book are current up to the beginning of 2021. The Knicks will surely topple more records and win more awards as the seasons pass, so keep this in mind when you're watching the next game with your friends, and someone starts a conversation with "Did you know…?".

CHAPTER 1:

ORIGINS & HISTORY

QUIZ TIME!

1. In which year did the Knicks begin playing in the National Basketball Association?

    a. 1946
    b. 1948
    c. 1952
    d. 1954

2. The franchise was nearly called the New York Dodgers, partially since New Yorkers walking down the streets needed to dodge oncoming streetcars, and partially to honor the beloved Brooklyn Dodgers baseball team that had moved to Los Angeles.

    a. True
    b. False

3. Which of the following details is NOT true about the origin of the nickname "Knickerbockers" that was chosen for the team?

a. It referred to a symbol of New York City known as "Father Knickerbocker" who was popular in the nineteenth and early twentieth centuries.

b. It was originally used in a famous novel written by American satirist Mark Twain.

c. It describes a type of pants worn with the legs rolled up to just under the knee.

d. It was selected by being drawn out of a hat by a small group of team officials.

4. The Knicks famously play their home games in Madison Square Garden in midtown Manhattan. Which version of the world famous arena is the one they currently play in?

   a. First version
   b. Second version
   c. Fourth version
   d. Seventh version

5. Who was the founder of the New York Knicks?

   a. Red Holzman
   b. Joe Lapchick
   c. Max Case
   d. Ned Irish

6. In which season did the Knicks earn their first-ever NBA championship?

   a. 1949-50
   b. 1959-60
   c. 1969-70
   d. 1979-80

7. Despite a 30-year stretch, from 1968 to 1998, without an NBA All-Star Game being played in New York, no other city has hosted more of these games than New York, which has held a total of five.

   a. True
   b. False

8. How many times in franchise history have the Knicks won a division title?

   a. 1
   b. 3
   c. 8
   d. 14

9. Which of the three reserves that the New York Knicks placed as representatives of the team at the first-ever NBA All-Star Game scored the most points in that contest?

   a. Guard Dick McGuire
   b. Forward Vince Boryla
   c. Center Harry Gallatin
   d. None of them scored during the game.

10. Where do the Knicks rank among NBA franchises when it comes to most Larry O'Brien Championship Trophies won?

    a. 1st overall
    b. Within the top five franchises
    c. Within the top 10 franchises
    d. Within the bottom 10 franchises

11. In 1956, the Knicks finished the regular season tied for the last playoff spot with the Syracuse Nationals. How was the tiebreaker that eliminated the Knicks from playoff contention determined?

    a. By the Nationals' better head-to-head record against the Knicks during the regular season
    b. By virtue of Syracuse scoring more total points during the regular season
    c. By a coin flip conducted by NBA Commissioner Maurice Podoloff
    d. By a tiebreaker play-in game, in which Syracuse defeated New York

12. The longest stretch the Knicks have gone without making the playoffs is seven years. This has occurred twice in team history, including a current streak which could become a new record of eight or more seasons.

    a. True
    b. False

13. Which team did New York face at home in 1947 in the first-ever NBA game played on Christmas Day (which resulted in an 89-75 Knicks victory)?

    a. Providence Steamrollers
    b. Boston Celtics
    c. Washington Bullets
    d. Kansas City Kings

14. What is the name of New York's current top development team that plays in the NBA G League?

a. Bronx Bombers

b. New York Baby Knicks

c. Westchester Knicks

d. Big Apple Empire

15. What was the outcome in the first NBA game ever played in which the New York Knicks faced off against the Toronto Huskies at Maple Leaf Gardens?

a. Huskies defeat Knicks, 40-34

b. Knicks defeat Huskies, 40-34

c. Knicks defeat Huskies, 68-66

d. Game ends in a draw, 55-55

16. As of 2020, New York is tied with the Los Angeles Lakers and Houston Rockets as the NBA franchises who have sent the most players to the Summer Olympics to represent their countries.

a. True

b. False

17. How did New York fare in its first-ever NBA playoff run?

a. Lost in the first round to the Baltimore Bullets

b. Lost in the division finals to the Syracuse Nationals

c. Lost in the semifinals to the Philadelphia Warriors

d. Lost in the NBA Finals to the Minneapolis Lakers

18. Hiring a person of which ethnicity made the New York Knicks employ the first ever non-Caucasian player in NBA history?

a. African-American

b. Mexican-American

c. Japanese-American

d. Native American

19. What is the name of the Knicks' mascot?

    a. Father Knickerbocker

    b. Big Apple Benny

    c. Ned York

    d. The Knicks do not have a mascot.

20. The Knicks have never in their history defeated the Boston Celtics in an NBA playoff series.

    a. True

    b. False

QUIZ ANSWERS

1. A – 1946
2. B – False
3. B – It was originally used in a famous novel written by American satirist Mark Twain.
4. C – Fourth version
5. D – Ned Irish
6. C – 1969-70
7. A – True
8. C – 8
9. B – Forward Vince Boryla
10. C – Within the top 10 franchises
11. D – By a tiebreaker play-in game, in which Syracuse defeated New York
12. A – True
13. A – Providence Steamrollers
14. C – Westchester Knicks
15. C – Knicks defeat Huskies, 68-66
16. B – False
17. C – Lost in the semifinals to the Philadelphia Warriors
18. C – Japanese-American
19. D – The Knicks do not have a mascot.
20. B – False

DID YOU KNOW?

1. As an original member team of the NBA, New York has fittingly not been shuffled around much during conference or division realignment. In fact, they have changed only once. The team has always played in the NBA's East Conference. From 1946 to 1969, they were in the Eastern Division, and since 1970, they have been slotted into the Atlantic Division.

2. The Knicks are not the only basketball team to play in their home state. New York City, as America's largest city, is also more than big enough to support the Brooklyn Nets, who play just over five miles away at the Barclays Center.

3. The Knicks were one of 11 original teams from 1946 to play in the league that would become the National Basketball Association. Only three of those original franchises remain in the league today, and since the Philadelphia Warriors moved to Golden State, only the Boston Celtics and New York Knicks retain both their original city and nickname.

4. While the Knicks are an anchor tenant of Madison Square Garden, it is not their home exclusively. The St. John's Red Storm plays NCAA basketball games there, and the arena configuration shrinks, losing about 1,800 seats, to house the National Hockey League's New York Rangers,

and expands by between 200-900 seats when musical acts or professional wrestling comes to town.

5. As a new team entering the NBA in 1946, the Knicks paid a $1,000 franchise fee for the right to join the league. Their original salary cap that year was $30,000. For context, when the Toronto Raptors joined in 1993, they paid an expansion fee of $125 million, and the NBA salary cap is currently just over $109 million.

6. During their inaugural season in the NBA, the Knicks finished with a winning record and even won a playoff round, despite the team's shooting percentage of just 28% for the year.

7. New York's biggest NBA rival is generally thought to be the Chicago Bulls, as the two cities have often competed for prominence in many areas. The basketball rivalry took off in the 1980s and '90s when both had strong teams and met in the playoffs several times. The Bulls have the advantage in the head-to-head rivalry, 140-110, and have also won more championships.

8. The Knicks are not fantastic when it comes to celebrating anniversaries. They have missed the playoffs during their 10th, 30th, 40th, 60th, and 70th anniversary seasons. In their 20th and 50th anniversaries, the team did qualify, but was defeated by the Boston Celtics and Miami Heat, respectively.

9. Team founder Ned Irish learned that he could make money during the Great Depression by promoting college

basketball games at the frequently available Madison Square Garden. Flush off of this success, Irish moved into the professional game and made the Knicks a charter member of the league that would eventually become the National Basketball Association.

10. In the beginning, the Knicks started very successfully. They began in 1946 and reeled off nine consecutive winning seasons. Recent history has not been so kind, as New York is currently riding a seven-season streak of finishing with a losing record.

CHAPTER 2:

JERSEYS & NUMBERS

QUIZ TIME!

1. When they began playing in the NBA in 1946, the Knicks used what color scheme for their home and away uniforms?

   a. Maroon and white

   b. Blue, green, and black

   c. Blue, orange, and white

   d. Black, white, and gray

2. The numbers 0 and 00 have been banned from circulation by New York's ownership, as they are seen to represent a losing attitude.

   a. True

   b. False

3. In which year did the Knicks debut an alternate uniform that used orange as the primary color for both the shorts and jersey?

   a. 2004

   b. 2009

c. 2013

d. 2018

4. Why do the modern-day Knicks use blue, white, and orange in their official logo and jerseys?

    a. Blue represents the water surrounding Manhattan Island, orange represents a basketball, and white was chosen as a highlight color.

    b. All three colors were chosen to match the design of the New York Mets baseball team.

    c. Founder Ned Irish also ran the Kinsey Corporation, which used a blue, white, and orange color scheme.

    d. Blue, white, and orange are the official colors of New York City.

5. Aside from the usual "New York" on their chests, what else have the Knicks occasionally sported on the front of their jerseys for Latin Nights?

    a. "Los Knicks"

    b. "Manzana Grande"

    c. "Harlem Globetrotters"

    d. "Nueva York"

6. Which jersey number has proven to be most popular with New York, having been worn by 28 players?

    a. 2

    b. 5

    c. 11

    d. 21

7. The highest number ever retired by the New York Knicks is number 24, belonging to forward Bill Bradley.

    a. True
    b. False

8. Who is the player to wear the highest numbered jersey in Knicks franchise history?

    a. Center Andrea Bargnani, number 77
    b. Guard Baron Davis, number 85
    c. Forward Mindaugas Kuzminskas, number 91
    d. Center Taj Gibson, number 99

9. Why did star Knicks forward Bernard King choose to wear number 30 on his jersey?

    a. He was 30 years old when he was acquired by New York.
    b. He wanted to average 30 points per game with the team.
    c. He liked round numbers, but numbers 10 and 20 were already taken.
    d. He wanted to honor pitcher Nolan Ryan, whom King considered the best athlete he had ever seen.

10. Swingman Shandon Anderson is the only Knick to ever wear which of the following uniform numbers?

    a. 49
    b. 28
    c. 46
    d. 77

11. Which unusual color have the Knicks worn occasionally to celebrate a specific holiday?

    a. Pink, to celebrate Valentine's Day
    b. Orange, to celebrate Halloween
    c. Green, to celebrate St. Patrick's Day
    d. Yellow, to celebrate Easter

12. Star center Patrick Ewing is the only Knick to have ever worn the number 33 on his jersey and will continue to be the only one as his number is now retired.

    a. True
    b. False

13. Which slogan did the Knicks choose to embroider into their jersey necklines for the 2012-13 NBA season?

    a. "It's Up To You, New York"
    b. "Five Are Stronger Than One"
    c. "Never Give Up"
    d. "Once A Knick, Always A Knick"

14. How many jersey numbers have the New York Knicks retired for their former players?

    a. 5
    b. 7
    c. 10
    d. 12

15. Which player competed for the Knicks for just six seasons; the shortest tenure of anyone whose number has been retired by the franchise?

a. Guard Earl Monroe

b. Forward Bill Bradley

c. Forward Dave DeBusschere

d. Center Willis Reed

16. Fourteen players have worn the number 1 for New York, and every single one of them was a point guard.

    a. True

    b. False

17. Lucky number 7 has been worn by 26 Knicks players over the years, but which lucky athlete got to wear it for the longest amount of time?

    a. Forward Carmelo Anthony

    b. Guard Dean Meminger

    c. Guard Gerald Henderson

    d. Guard Ray Lumpp

18. Who is the most recent Knicks player to have his number retired by the club?

    a. Guard John Starks

    b. Center Patrick Ewing

    c. Center Willis Reed

    d. Forward Dave DeBusschere

19. Which of the following has NOT been included on one of the New York Knicks' "City" uniforms, designed to pay homage to local culture?

    a. A firefighter, ladder, and hydrant in a nod to New York firefighters

b. The phrase "City Never Sleeps" in reference to one of New York's nicknames

c. A depiction of the New York City skyline

d. Five stars surrounding a basketball, symbolizing the five boroughs of New York

20. During the 1970s, the Knicks agreed to a participate in a game against the Detroit Pistons without wearing jerseys. The game was marketed as "Shirts vs. Skins" and was a major success as a publicity stunt.

a. True

b. False

QUIZ ANSWERS

1. C – Blue, orange, and white

2. B – False

3. C – 2013

4. D – Blue, white, and orange are the official colors of New York City.

5. D – "Nueva York"

6. B – 5

7. B – False

8. C – Forward Mindaugas Kuzminskas, number 91

9. B – He wanted to average 30 points per game with the team.

10. A – 49

11. C – Green, to celebrate St. Patrick's Day

12. B – False

13. D – "Once A Knick, Always A Knick"

14. B – 7

15. C – Forward Dave DeBusschere

16. B – False

17. A – Forward Carmelo Anthony

18. B – Center Patrick Ewing

19. D – Five stars surrounding a basketball, symbolizing the five boroughs of New York

20. B – False

DID YOU KNOW?

1. The Knicks have cycled through multiple logos during their existence. They began with one featuring "Father Knickerbocker," a New York figure dribbling a basketball. In 1964, the team switched to a "Roundball" logo, displaying the team's name on a basketball. In 1992, New York superimposed their name and a basketball in front of a triangle, which remains the basis for the team's current logo.

2. In an amusing mistake during a 2020 game against the Philadelphia 76ers, Knicks swingman Reggie Bullock played with his number 25 on the front of his jersey, but the number 23 on the back. Since center Mitchell Robinson was already wearing 23, Bullock had to discard the jersey and put on a fresh one.

3. Though the Knicks are a charter franchise of the NBA, it was not until 2013 that one of their players officially recorded the top-selling jersey in the league. This honor belonged to forward Carmelo Anthony, whose number 7 was the most popular with fans that year.

4. Some numbers have proven unpopular with New York players. Forty-eight numbers have gone unused in franchise history, as no Knick has ever worn a jersey with the following numbers: 27, 29, 37, 38, 39, 47, 48, 53, 56, 57, 58, 59, 60, 61, 62, 63, 64, 65, 66, 68, 69, 70, 71, 72, 73, 74, 75,

76, 78, 79, 80, 81, 82, 83, 84, 86, 87, 88, 89, 90, 92, 93, 94, 95, 96, 97, 98, or 99.

5. New York has retired a very unusual number, which hangs in the rafters at Madison Square Garden: 613. That number was chosen to represent coach Red Holzman's contributions to the franchise, as Holzman won 613 games while coaching the Knicks.

6. Seven players have worn number 0 for the Knicks, but only one has ever donned 00 on his back. This was Turkish center Enes Kanter, who wore the unique set of digits from 2018 to 2019.

7. Superstition may have scared some Knicks away from wearing the number 13. Only fourteen players in franchise history have chosen it for themselves, and no one wore it during the team's first three decades in existence.

8. No Knick has ever worn a jersey with a number higher than 55 for longer than three seasons before switching numbers or leaving the team.

9. The number 15 has been retired in honor of two separate Knicks guards. Dick McGuire played for the team during the 1950s, and Earl Monroe took the court for New York in the 1970s. Interestingly, the team chose to retire the number for Monroe first, six years before honoring McGuire.

10. For special games, the Knicks have used a secondary logo designed to look like a subway token. This logo is a yellow circle surrounded by blue trim, with the letters "NYK" written in black on the inside.

CHAPTER 3:

CATCHY NICKNAMES

QUIZ TIME!

1. By which nickname was Knicks great Willis Reed most commonly referred to?

   a. "New York Wille"
   b. "The Big Bossman"
   c. "Mr. Knick"
   d. "The Captain"

2. Feisty Knicks guard John Starks was often referred to as "Johnny Knock-Out" thanks to his toughness and refusal to back down whenever opposing players challenged him on the court.

   a. True
   b. False

3. Current Knicks center Mitchell Robinson goes by which of the following nicknames that reference his defensive prowess?

   a. "The Rejecter"

b. "Shut Down Mitch"

c. "The Block Ness Monster"

d. "Papa Protector"

4. In 2019, Knicks center DeAndre Jordan was dubbed "DeAndre 3000," in reference to a rapper from which popular hip hop group?

a. Wu-Tang Clan

b. Public Enemy

c. A Tribe Called Quest

d. OutKast

5. Why was star Knicks point guard Walt Frazer nicknamed "Clyde"?

a. Because his father, also an NBA player (though not a star), was named Clyde.

b. Because the Knicks public address announcer liked to yell "Frazer glides to the hoop!" but his teammates heard "glide" as "Clyde."

c. Because his jump shot reminded coaches of famous Harlem Globetrotter Clyde "Long Ball" Johnson's shooting stroke.

d. Because he wore a fedora like the character Clyde Barrow did in the hit movie *Bonnie and Clyde*.

6. Which of the following is NOT a nickname that was given to Knicks guard Jamal Crawford for his notable scoring capabilities?

a. "Crawssover Crawford"

b. "Mr. And-One"

c. "The Ankle-Breaker"

d. "J-Crossover"

7. Knicks center Amar'e Stoudemire used an acronym as his preferred nickname. Stoudemire went by "STAT," which did not refer to statistics, as many assumed, but stood for "Standing Tall and Talented."

a. True

b. False

8. Why was center Harry Gallatin given the nickname "The Horse" by teammates on the Knicks?

a. Because of the awkward way he galloped down the court

b. Because of the huge amount of food he consumed before and after games

c. Because of his strength, despite being undersized for the position

d. Because he was impossible to defeat at the shooting game HORSE

9. During the short period of time in 2012 known as "Linsanity," wherein point guard Jeremy Lin became a starter for New York, which of the following did NOT happen to Lin?

a. Seven e-books were published about him within a three-week period.

b. Knicks owner James Dolan offered Lin private use of his mega yacht, Cable Buoy.

c. He appeared on the cover of *Time* and *Sports Illustrated* magazines, including twice in a row on the latter.

d. A frozen yogurt flavor featuring fortune cookie chunks and lychee honey called "Taste the Lin-Sanity" was created by Ben & Jerry's.

10. For what reason did Knicks fans refer to power forward Larry Johnson as "Grandmama"?

    a. His grandmother attended every Knicks game, sitting courtside in the seats Johnson had secured for her.

    b. He moved terribly slowly up and down the court, at the speed of a senior citizen.

    c. He was fanatic about making chicken soup for any teammate who came down with an illness during the season, swearing it would cure their cold.

    d. He played a character by that name in a series of popular Converse commercials.

11. Which Knicks player was known to fans and teammates by the two nicknames "The Skull" and "Fall Back Baby"?

    a. Guard Allan Houston

    b. Forward Anthony Mason

    c. Guard Dick Barnett

    d. Guard John Starks

12. After engaging in two memorable fights with his former New York Knicks teammates as a newly traded member of the Boston Celtics, forward Xavier McDaniel earned the nickname "The Vengeful X."

a. True

b. False

13. Which Knick is known to teammates by the nickname "Crobe," which is a shortened version of "Croatian Kobe," thanks to the player's heritage and idolization of Los Angeles Lakers superstar Kobe Bryant?

   a. Forward Ignas Brazdeikis
   b. Swingman Mario Hezonja
   c. Forward Obi Toppin
   d. Guard Frank Ntilikina

14. Why did teammates call Knicks forward Carmelo Anthony by the nicknames "Captain America" and "The Patriot"?

   a. He wore a Captain America costume to a Knicks Halloween party during his first year with the team.
   b. He stood silently at rigid attention during the national anthem before games.
   c. He frequently represented Team USA in international competitions.
   d. He has a tattoo of the American flag across his back and shoulders.

15. At times during his basketball career, Knicks guard Earl Monroe was referred to by all of the following nicknames except for which one?

   a. "Mr. Mayor"
   b. "Earl the Pearl"

c. "Black Jesus"

d. "Thomas Edison"

16. Knicks center Dikembe Mutombo was called "The Guru" by his young teammates because he was brought in to provide leadership and playoff experience while demonstrating how to act as a professional athlete.

a. True

b. False

17. Which famous Harlem Globetrotter joined the Knicks for several years after the team saw his incredible ball control skills?

a. Nathaniel "Sweetwater" Clifton

b. Reece "Goose" Tatum

c. Meadow "Meadowlark" Lemon

d. Fred "Curly" Neal

18. Knicks forward and future general manager Phil Jackson was given several nicknames during his long NBA career, which of the following is NOT one of his nicknames?

a. "The Mop"

b. "The Zen Master"

c. "The Happy Hooker"

d. "Encyclopedia Jackson"

19. Which of the following is NOT an actual Knicks player reference in a song lyric from New York rap rock group the Beastie Boys?

a. "I'm like Al Goldstein / Yeah I'm all about screwing / Lead my team to 60 wins / Like my man Pat Ewing"

b. "Got another little story that I like to retell / Comin' quick and hard at ya like Latrell Sprewell"

c. "I got my hair cut correct like Anthony Mason / Then I ride the IRT right up to Penn Station"

d. "More updated on the hip hop lingo / My favorite New York Knick was Harthorne Wingo"

20. Although he played three years with the Knicks at the beginning of his career, shooting guard Dick Van Arsdale was plucked from New York by the Phoenix Suns in the 1968 NBA Expansion Draft, and thus became known as "The Original Sun."

    a. True
    b. False

QUIZ ANSWERS

1. D – "The Captain"

2. B – False

3. C – "The Block Ness Monster"

4. D – OutKast

5. D – Because he wore a fedora like the character Clyde Barrow did in the hit movie *Bonnie and Clyde*.

6. C – "The Ankle-Breaker"

7. A – True

8. C – Because of his strength, despite being undersized for the position

9. B – Knicks owner James Dolan offered Lin private use of his mega yacht, Cable Buoy.

10. D – He played a character by that name in a series of popular Converse commercials.

11. C – Guard Dick Barnett

12. B – False

13. B – Swingman Mario Hezonja

14. C – He frequently represented Team USA in international competitions.

15. A – "Mr. Mayor"

16. B – False

17. A – Nathaniel "Sweetwater" Clifton

18. D – "Encyclopedia Jackson"

19. B – "Got another little story that I like to retell / Comin' quick and hard at ya like Latrell Sprewell"

20. A – True

DID YOU KNOW?

1. Imposing power forward/center Kurt Thomas had a long career that began in 1995, ended in 2013, and included two stints with the Knicks. His nicknames evolved over the course of his career. At the beginning, he was known as "Big Sexy" by those who liked him, and "Dirty Kurt" by those who didn't. As he turned 40 years old in his last season in New York, though, teammates took to calling him "Mid Life" instead.

2. It is so commonly used that many people assume that Knicks guard "Doc" Rivers goes by his actual name. Rivers is actually Glenn Anton Rivers, but got the nickname in college at Marquette when a coach saw him wearing a T-shirt featuring superstar Julius "Dr. J" Erving on the front and called Rivers "Doc." The name still sticks, decades later.

3. One Knicks guard's nickname spawned a nickname for another. Steve "The Franchise" Francis suited up for New York in 2006-07. When Frank Ntilikina, who grew up in France, ended up in New York a decade later, he was dubbed "The Frenchise."

4. After losing to Earl Monroe's Baltimore Bullets in the 1971 NBA playoffs, New York acquired Monroe in a trade and paired him with fellow guard Walt Frazier on the court,

where the duo was known as "The Rolls Royce Backcourt" for their star power and ability.

5. Forward Bill Bradley was known by a few nicknames in New York. Depending on who was describing him, he could be known as "Dollar Bill," "The Secretary of State," or "Mr. President."

6. New York born and raised guard Stephon Marbury was ticketed for stardom at an early age. Long before he made it big in the NBA and excelled for the Knicks, he was called "Starbury" in many media publications. Marbury even named his clothing line "Starbury," and famously sold shoes at much more affordable prices than larger companies.

7. Two Italian players who have suited up for the Knicks naturally have Italian nicknames. Center Andrea Bargnani was called "Il Mago" ("The Magician"), and Danilo Gallinari was dubbed "Il Gallo" ("The Rooster").

8. Aside from its simpler, short-form nicknames such as "MSG" or "The Garden," the home of the Knicks, Madison Square Garden, is also known as "The Mecca of Basketball" and "The World's Most Famous Arena."

9. Knicks forward Carmelo Anthony goes by the short form "Melo," but his wife Alani Vazquez is perhaps more famous for her nickname "La La." When the two were married in 2010, the occasion was marked with a reality television show called *La La's Full Court Wedding*.

10. Franchise legend Patrick Ewing was never given a memorable moniker while with the Knicks, usually going by just "Pat" or "Big Pat." In his college days at Georgetown, however, he was known by the much catchier "Hoya Destroya."

CHAPTER 4:

ALMA MATERS

QUIZ TIME!

1. Hall of Fame guard Richie Guerin was not as highly scouted as many other players, because he attended which little-known college?

   a. University of Tennessee at Chattanooga
   b. Iona College
   c. Truman State University
   d. Pikeville College

2. The Knicks have drafted precisely the same number of players from the Michigan State Spartans as they have from the Michigan Wolverines over the course of their history.

   a. True
   b. False

3. Point guard Henry "Instant Offense" Bibby played four years of college ball for which West Coast program before being drafted by the Knicks?

a. Pepperdine University Waves

b. Stanford University Cardinals

c. University of California Golden Bears

d. University of California-Los Angeles Bruins

4. First-ever Knicks draft choice Dick Holub attended Long Island University, where he played for the basketball team that went by which nickname?

a. Islanders

b. Pilgrims

c. Sharks

d. Minutemen

5. From which of the following college basketball programs have the Knicks drafted the most players?

a. Texas Longhorns

b. Texas A&M Aggies

c. Texas Tech Red Raiders

d. Texas El Paso Miners

6. Sensational Knicks point guard Jeremy Lin graduated from which prestigious college, before going unselected in the NBA Draft?

a. Massachusetts Institute of Technology

b. Stanford University

c. Harvard University

d. Johns Hopkins University

7. Fan favorite power forward David Lee is the only player the Knicks have ever selected who played in college for the University of Florida Gators.

a. True

b. False

8. Knicks center Patrick Ewing had a strong bond with players who attended his alma mater, Georgetown University. Which Hoyas teammate did Ewing offer to donate a kidney to, even going so far as to be tested to check his compatibility?

   a. Guard Allen Iverson
   b. Forward Michael Sweetney
   c. Center Alonzo Mourning
   d. Center Dikembe Mutombo

9. The Knicks selected two sets of college teammates in the 1968 NBA Draft in Don May and Bobby Hooper and Pat Moriarty and Ed Fellers from which schools?

   a. University of Dayton and Guilford College
   b. Ohio State University and University of South Carolina
   c. St. Francis College and University of the Pacific
   d. United States Military Academy and University of Arkansas at Pine Bluff

10. Top overall pick Cazzie Russell played his college basketball as the small forward for which program before coming to the Knicks in 1966?

   a. University of North Carolina Tar Heels
   b. University of Kentucky Wildcats
   c. University of Wisconsin Badgers
   d. University of Michigan Wolverines

11. Only two Ivy League players have played for the Knicks after being drafted by them. Which intelligent players made it with New York?

   a. James Salters of University of Pennsylvania and Ed Peterson of Cornell University
   b. Ed Smith of Harvard University and Bill Bradley of Princeton University
   c. Dennis Lynch of Yale University and Andy Michasiow of Brown University
   d. Roger Walaszak of Columbia University and Shawn Bradley of Dartmouth University

12. Knicks draftee Greg Anthony gave up his scholarship at the University of Nevada-Las Vegas because he ran his own T-shirt business and could afford to pay the tuition himself.

   a. True
   b. False

13. Guard Shane Larkin was drafted by the Knicks in 2013 out of which school that is better known as a football powerhouse than a basketball school?

   a. University of Miami
   b. Clemson University
   c. Louisiana State University
   d. University of Alabama

14. The Knicks drafted two players from the University of Indiana Hoosiers who would go on to play more than 750 NBA games each. Who were these players?

a. Center Kurt Rambis and swingman Gerald Wilkins

b. Center Darrall Imhoff and forward Barry Clemens

c. Guard Ray Williams and forward Walter McCarty

d. Guards Dick Van Arsdale and Mike Woodson

15. Which historically black college was attended by Knicks center Willis Reed from 1960 to 1964?

a. Xavier University

b. Grambling State University

c. Howard University

d. Florida A&M University

16. Center Paul Hogue, who was chosen 2nd overall in 1962, is the only drafted player the Knicks have ever selected from the University of Cincinnati Bearcats.

a. True

b. False

17. Which colorful college program did Syracuse, New York born, Canadian national team guard Andy Rautins (who holds dual citizenship) attend before his entrance into the NBA with a 2010 draft selection by the Knicks?

a. Syracuse University Orange

b. University of Toronto Varsity Blues

c. University of North Texas Mean Green

d. St. John's University Red Storm

18. The most recent players who were teammates in college before taking the court together after being drafted to the Knicks were which of the following duos?

a. Guards Tim Hardaway and Iman Shumpert at the University of Michigan

b. Center Patrick Ewing and guard Michael Jackson at Georgetown University

c. Forwards John Wallace and Carmelo Anthony at Syracuse University

d. Forward Lonnie Shelton and guard Michael Ray Richardson at Oregon State University

19. The high-scoring Bill Cartwright was a member of which college squad before his time on the court with the Knicks?

a. University of California-Los Angeles Bruins

b. University of Connecticut Huskies

c. University of San Francisco Dons

d. University of Maryland Terrapins

20. Due in part to their longstanding rivalry with the Boston Celtics, New York has never drafted a player from the Boston College Eagles.

a. True

b. False

QUIZ ANSWERS

1. B – Iona College

2. A – True

3. D – University of California-Los Angeles Bruins

4. C – Sharks

5. C – Texas Tech Red Raiders

6. C – Harvard University

7. B – False

8. C – Center Alonzo Mourning

9. A – University of Dayton and Guilford College

10. D – University of Michigan Wolverines

11. B – Ed Smith of Harvard University and Bill Bradley of Princeton University

12. A – True

13. A – University of Miami

14. D – Guards Dick Van Arsdale and Mike Woodson

15. B – Grambling State University

16. B – False

17. A – Syracuse University Orange

18. B – Center Patrick Ewing and guard Michael Jackson at Georgetown University

19. C – University of San Francisco Dons

20. A – True

DID YOU KNOW?

1. Prior to his standout NBA career, Knicks guard John Starks attended four different colleges in the state of Oklahoma, including Rogers State College, Northern Oklahoma College, Tulsa Junior College, and Oklahoma State University. A series of criminal incidents led to this shuffling around and caused Starks to go undrafted before joining the league as a free agent.

2. New York has made two Duke University Blue Devils players top three picks in the NBA Draft. The team selected swingman Art Heyman 1st overall in 1963 and shooting guard R.J. Barrett 3rd overall in 2019.

3. In 2006, Knicks forward Carmelo Anthony made one of the most expensive donations ever by an athlete to his former college, Syracuse University. Anthony, who had spent just one year at the school (in which he won an NCAA Championship), donated $3 million to fund a practice complex known as the Carmelo K. Anthony Basketball Center.

4. Point guard Charlie Ward remains the only Florida State Seminole ever taken by the New York Knicks in an NBA Draft. Ward was a dual sport star in college, and actually won the 1993 Heisman Trophy as the best college football player in the country.

5. Two future New York Knicks won an NCAA Championship with the UNLV Runnin' Rebels in 1990. Point guard Greg Anthony and power forward Larry Johnson were both leaders on the team, and Anthony set an amazing example of toughness by playing most of the season while his jaw was broken.

6. While starring at Georgetown University, future Knicks center Patrick Ewing led the Hoyas to three NCAA Championship games, winning one title and being named the Final Four's Most Outstanding Player in 1984.

7. The Knicks have hit on three strong players out of DePaul University over the years. Point guard Em Bryant was taken in 1964, followed by another point guard, Rod Strickland, in 1988, and forward Wilson Chandler in 2007.

8. Perhaps the most impressive Knick of all time academically, guard Bill Bradley turned down 75 scholarship offers to play for the Ivy League's Princeton University Tigers. After his graduation there, he received a Rhodes Scholarship and went on to further studies at Oxford University in England before finally joining New York's NBA team in 1967.

9. Knicks stalwart Patrick Ewing was a star for Georgetown University in the 1980s. His son, Patrick Ewing Jr., also went to Georgetown after transferring from the University of Indiana in 2005. Ewing Jr. never made it to the NBA, despite being named as an all-star in the NBA's Development League.

10. Before leading the Knicks to two NBA championships, guard Walt Frazier played college ball for the Southern Illinois Salukis. Frazier helped the Salukis to the 1967 NIT championship, in what was the last college basketball matchup ever held at the old version of Madison Square Garden.

CHAPTER 5:

STATISTICALLY SPEAKING

QUIZ TIME!

1. What is New York's franchise record for most victories recorded by the club in a single regular season?

    a. 55
    b. 58
    c. 60
    d. 63

2. No one in Knicks history is within 1,000 assists of Walt Frazier at the top of New York's record book.

    a. True
    b. False

3. Who of the five players that have recorded over 5,000 career rebounds for the Knicks has recorded the most?

    a. Forward Charles Oakley
    b. Center Willis Reed
    c. Forward Willie Naulls
    d. Center Patrick Ewing

4. Who is the Knicks' single-season leader in points scored, with 2,347?

   a. Guard Richie Guerin
   b. Forward Carmelo Anthony
   c. Center Patrick Ewing
   d. Forward Bernard King

5. Which Knick really made his shots count, showing his accuracy with .704 shooting; the highest career shooting percentage for the team and the only instance of a player shooting over .700?

   a. Center Mitchell Robinson
   b. Center Patrick Ewing
   c. Center Tyson Chandler
   d. Center Enes Kanter

6. The most fouls committed by a Knicks player in any season is 363, established by which aggressive player for the club record?

   a. Forward Kurt Thomas
   b. Center Willis Reed
   c. Center Patrick Ewing
   d. Forward Lonnie Shelton

7. Center Patrick Ewing has attempted more than double the number of career free throws for the Knicks as guard Walt Frazier, who is in second place on the franchise list.

   a. True
   b. False

8. Iconic center Patrick Ewing holds the New York record for most blocks in a single season, with 327 shots swatted away. How many of the Knicks' top 10 season totals for blocks does Ewing own?

   a. 2
   b. 5
   c. 9
   d. 10

9. Which Knicks member has played more NBA games with the franchise than any other player?

   a. Center Patrick Ewing
   b. Forward Bill Bradley
   c. Guard Trent Tucker
   d. Forward Phil Jackson

10. The talented John Starks is New York's all-time leader in three-point field goals scored, scoring how many?

    a. 705
    b. 982
    c. 1,141
    d. 1,205

11. Holding the single season record for points per game, how many points did the dynamic Bernard King average per game during that 1984-85 season?

    a. 29.7
    b. 31.5
    c. 32.9
    d. 38.3

12. Center Patrick Ewing has *missed* more field goals during his Knicks career than iconic New York forwards Bill Bradley or Carmelo Anthony have even *attempted*.

   a. True
   b. False

13. Which Knicks shooter sank the most free throws while playing with the club?

   a. Guard Walt Frazier
   b. Forward Harry Gallatin
   c. Guard Carl Braun
   d. Center Patrick Ewing

14. On the Knicks' top 10 list for points scored by a player in a season, how many times does forward Carmelo Anthony's name appear?

   a. 1
   b. 4
   c. 6
   d. 7

15. How many Knicks have fired over 10,000 field goal attempts for the club during their careers?

   a. 1
   b. 4
   c. 6
   d. 7

16. Guard John Starks hit 217 three-pointers during the 1994-95 season, which remains a franchise record.

a. True

b. False

17. Which New York player recorded the highest career three-point shooting percentage with the Knicks, with .449?

a. Forward Steve Novak

b. Forward Marcus Morris

c. Guard Hubert Davis

d. Guard Jose Calderon

18. Which Knick recorded the most rebounds in one season for the team, when he grabbed 1,191 loose balls for the squad?

a. Center Patrick Ewing

b. Center Walt Bellamy

c. Forward Charles Oakley

d. Center Willis Reed

19. Which two teammates posted the highest combined steals total in a season for the Knicks, snatching 432 balls away from their opponents?

a. Michael Ray Richardson and Ray Williams

b. Walt Frazier and Earl Monroe

c. John Starks and Chris Childs

d. Mark Jackson and Darrell Walker

20. Coach Pat Riley's 1993-94 season is the Knicks' benchmark in terms of winning percentage, as he led the team to a .695 winning percentage in the regular season.

a. True

b. False

QUIZ ANSWERS

1. C – 60

2. B – False

3. D – Center Patrick Ewing

4. C – Center Patrick Ewing

5. A – Center Mitchell Robinson

6. D – Forward Lonnie Shelton

7. B – False

8. C – 9

9. A – Center Patrick Ewing

10. B – 982

11. C – 32.9

12. A – True

13. D – Center Patrick Ewing

14. A – 1

15. B – 4

16. A – True

17. C – Guard Hubert Davis

18. D – Center Willis Reed

19. A – Michael Ray Richardson and Ray Williams

20. B – False

DID YOU KNOW?

1. Seven players have scored more than 10,000 points with the Knicks franchise. Forward Carmelo Anthony was the most recent to reach that milestone, but he remains more than 13,000 points behind Patrick Ewing atop the leaderboard.

2. Knicks icon Patrick Ewing ranks 23rd on the all-time list for most points in the NBA. His 24,815 points are the closest to 25,000 without reaching the mark, slightly ahead of Ray Allen and Allen Iverson.

3. The Knicks franchise legend Patrick Ewing still stands as the player who has contributed to the most victories in team history. Ewing accumulated 123 win shares over the course of his career, almost 15 more than Walt Frazier, who is second in New York's history.

4. Center Patrick Ewing was a force in the paint for the Knicks. Ewing blocked 2,758 shots during his New York career to lead the franchise in that statistic. He is more than 2,000 blocks ahead of his nearest competitor.

5. New York's record for the most points scored in a single game by any player is 62, set by forward Carmelo Anthony on January 13, 2004, against the Charlotte Bobcats. No visiting player has ever scored more against the Knicks either; Anthony owns the Madison Square Garden record as well.

6. Two players who starred together in New York's frontcourt hold the Knicks' career rebounding records. While forward Charles Oakley grabbed the most offensive boards with 2,580, center Patrick Ewing took down more defensive and total rebounds, with 8,191 and 10,759, respectively.

7. Center Bob McAdoo and guard Walt Frazier hold the top spots in the Knicks' record books when it comes to minutes per game. The indefatigable McAdoo averaged 39.8 minutes per game during his Knicks career, but Frazier had the most impressive season, averaging 43.2 minutes for the club in 1970-71.

8. The most recent time the Knicks sank more than 800 three-pointers in a season was 2018-19, when they tallied 823. This was not far off from the team record, 891, set in 2012-13.

9. Two Knicks players are tied for the title of deadliest free throw shooter. Guard Mike Glenn and forward Kiki Vandeweghe both shot a team record .886 from the stripe for New York. Vandeweghe's marks is slightly more impressive though, as he stretched out this strong shooting over nearly twice as many attempts.

10. In 1961-62, Richie Guerin had the green light and fired 1,897 shots, which established the Knicks' record for most shots taken by one player in a single season. He scored 839 times, which was good for a .442 shooting percentage.

CHAPTER 6:

THE TRADE MARKET

QUIZ TIME!

1. The Knicks struck it rich in a deal with the Baltimore Braves in 1976, netting Hall of Fame center Bob McAdoo in exchange for which lesser center?

   a. Daniel Taylor
   b. Eric Adams
   c. Tom McMillen
   d. John Gianelli

2. New York has never in its history completed a trade with the Miami Heat.

   a. True
   b. False

3. In 2000, the Knicks traded star center Patrick Ewing to the Seattle SuperSonics as part of a four-team trade, receiving who in exchange?

   a. Guard Emanual Davis, forward Chuck Person, and big men Greg Foster and Horace Grant

b. Forward Vin Baker and guards Jeff Green and Kareem Rush

c. Forward Glen Rice and centers Travis Knight and Luc Longley

d. Forward Lazaro Borrell, guard Vernon Maxwell, and center Vladimir Stepania

4. New York once held the draft pick that was used to take Hall of Fame forward Scottie Pippen, before trading it to which team in a deal that netted them guards Gerald Henderson and Mark Jackson?

a. New Jersey Nets

b. Chicago Bulls

c. Indiana Pacers

d. Seattle SuperSonics

5. Which useful Knicks player was NOT dealt to the Golden State Warriors in 1999 in exchange for star guard Latrell Sprewell?

a. Forward Terry Cummings

b. Guard John Starks

c. Guard Chris Childs

d. Forward Chris Mills

6. Which of the following superstars has NOT been involved in a trade between the Knicks and the Phoenix Suns?

a. Center Amar'e Stoudemire

b. Forward Charles Barkley

c. Guard Stephon Marbury

d. Forward Maurice Lucas

7. New York has completed more trades with the St. Louis / Atlanta Hawks franchise than with any other NBA franchise.

   a. True
   b. False

8. Who did the Knicks give up in order to pry popular power forward Larry Johnson away from the Charlotte Hornets in 1996?

   a. Forward Glen Rice and center Matt Geiger
   b. Guard Doug Christie and center Antonio Davis
   c. Forward Anthony Mason and center Brad Lohaus
   d. Forward Jerry Stackhouse and guard Dell Curry

9. Which of the following stars was NOT involved in a 2003 four-team trade between the Knicks, Philadelphia 76ers, Minnesota Timberwolves, and Atlanta Hawks in which New York traded troubled swingman Latrell Sprewell?

   a. Forward Glenn Robinson
   b. Forward Keith Van Horn
   c. Guard Terrell Brandon
   d. Center Brad Miller

10. As of 2020, the New York Knicks and Detroit Pistons have not made a trade in over how long?

    a. 5 years
    b. 10 years
    c. 20 years
    d. 30 years

11. Which high profile players dealt in a trade from the Baltimore Bullets to the Knicks franchise went on to be elected to the Hall of Fame?

    a. Center Walt Bellamy and guard Earl Monroe
    b. Forward Dave DeBusschere and center Dikembe Mutombo
    c. Guard Walt Frazier and center Bob McAdoo
    d. Guard Dick Barnett and forwards Bernard King and Spencer Haywood

12. New York has never in its history completed a trade with the Brooklyn Nets, due in part to the teams' close proximity and heavy media coverage.

    a. True
    b. False

13. The Knicks went over 40 years between trades with one franchise; so long that the team had relocated in the interim. Which franchise did New York go through this long dormant stretch with?

    a. The Kansas City / Sacramento Kings
    b. The Philadelphia / Golden State Warriors
    c. The New Orleans / Utah Jazz
    d. The Minneapolis / Los Angeles Lakers

14. Knicks executive Isiah Thomas traded away two lottery picks to Chicago to obtain young center Eddy Curry. Which two better players did those lottery picks turn out to be?

a. Center Tyson Chandler and guard Derrick Rose

b. Centers LaMarcus Aldridge and Joakim Noah

c. Forward Luol Deng and Lauri Markkanen

d. Guards Ben Gordon and Kirk Hinrich

15. New York maximized its return on point guard Mark Jackson, not only getting great play from him on the court, but also dealing him not only once but twice, to which other NBA franchise(s)?

a. Indiana Pacers and Utah Jazz

b. Toronto Raptors and Houston Rockets

c. Twice to the Indiana Pacers

d. Los Angeles Clippers and Denver Nuggets

16. The Knicks have made more trades with the Charlotte Hornets than the Charlotte Bobcats.

a. True

b. False

17. When the Knicks needed to deal forward Carmelo Anthony away from New York in 2017 because of Anthony's trade demand, which franchise did they send him to in order to resolve his dispute with team president Phil Jackson?

a. Portland Trail Blazers

b. Houston Rockets

c. Oklahoma City Thunder

d. Cleveland Cavaliers

18. Which player did New York send out in return after acquiring former 1ˢᵗ overall pick Darko Milicic from the Memphis Grizzlies in 2009?

    a. Swingman Quentin Richardson
    b. Forward Wilson Chandler
    c. Center Jerome James
    d. Guard Chris Duhon

19. In 2004, the Knicks completed a large three-team trade, acquiring center Nazr Mohammed and forward Tim Thomas. The team sent out center Michael Doleac, forward Keith Van Horn, and a 2ⁿᵈ round draft pick. Who were the other two teams involved in the complicated deal?

    a. New Jersey Nets and Houston Rockets
    b. Utah Jazz and Dallas Mavericks
    c. Atlanta Hawks and Milwaukee Bucks
    d. Cleveland Cavaliers and Boston Celtics

20. Knicks General Manager Ernie Grunfeld once proposed a deal to the Chicago Bulls that would have sent Knicks icon Patrick Ewing to the Windy City in exchange for a young Michael Jordan.

    a. True
    b. False

QUIZ ANSWERS

1. D – John Gianelli

2. B – False

3. C – Forward Glen Rice and centers Travis Knight and Luc Longley

4. D – Seattle SuperSonics

5. C – Guard Chris Childs

6. B – Forward Charles Barkley

7. A – True

8. C – Forward Anthony Mason and center Brad Lohaus

9. D – Center Brad Miller

10. D – 30 years

11. A – Center Walt Bellamy and guard Earl Monroe

12. B – False

13. C – The New Orleans / Utah Jazz

14. B – Centers LaMarcus Aldridge and Joakim Noah

15. D – Los Angeles Clippers and Denver Nuggets

16. A – True

17. C – Oklahoma City Thunder

18. A – Swingman Quentin Richardson

19. C – Atlanta Hawks and Milwaukee Bucks

20. B – False

DID YOU KNOW?

1. New York has never sent an actual player to the New Orleans Pelicans. They have made a single trade with New Orleans, in 2011, in which they acquired big man Josh Harrellson in exchange for financial considerations.

2. The Knicks and Chicago Bulls have had a fairly heated rivalry throughout their existence, particularly during the 1980s and '90s. The two teams have set aside their dislike for each other to make a trade nine times in New York's long tenure in the NBA, though, swapping important players like Derrick Rose, Tim Thomas, Larry Hughes, Jamal Crawford, Dikembe Mutombo, Charles Oakley, and Bill Cartwright.

3. In what, by volume, was one of the Knicks' largest trades ever, New York made a monstrous deal with the Minnesota Timberwolves and Denver Nuggets in 2011, with their primary goal being to bring in star forward Carmelo Anthony. The swap saw 13 players switch cities, along with six draft picks, two rights to draft pick swaps, and cash changing hands.

4. New York and Houston have a rich history of trades throughout the years, completing nine separate deals. Significant names moved between the two teams include: Tracy McGrady, Patrick Ewing, Vin Baker, and Glen Rice.

5. The Knicks and Boston Celtics have each been part of the NBA for 75 years. During all that time, the teams have only made three trades with each other, in 1979, 1997, and 2010.

6. It is unusual to trade a coach in the NBA, but the Knicks have made two such swaps in under a decade. In 1995, they sent Pat Riley to the Miami Heat, and in 2003, they dealt Jeff Van Gundy to the Houston Rockets. Evidently, Riley was the better coach, as he fetched a 1st round draft pick, while Van Gundy only earned the Knicks a 2nd round pick.

7. One of the worst trades made by the Knicks occurred in 2013 when they sent center Marcus Camby, forward Steve Novak, swingman Quentin Richardson, one 1st round draft pick, and two 2nd round draft picks to the Toronto Raptors for center Andrea Bargnani. Bargnani struggled defensively, was frequently injured, and his massive contract was a drag on New York's salary cap for years to come.

8. The Dallas Mavericks were generally a good team to work with when New York needed to make a trade. The two teams have combined on nine trades in their history, but it was not until 2014 when Dallas got the better end of a deal (as measured by the win shares of the players received). Even in that deal, Dallas received center Tyson Chandler, whom they had previously regretted trading to the Knicks.

9. In a deal that was very unpopular at the time (2002), New York dealt point guard Mark Jackson and centers Marcus Camby and Nene to the Denver Nuggets for forward Antonio McDyess and guard Frank Williams. Neither McDyess nor Williams lasted a full 82-game season playing for the Knicks, while Camby and Nene went on to play over 900 games for Denver.

10. One of the larger and more impactful trades ever made by the Knicks was completed October 4, 2005, with the Chicago Bulls. Chicago sent Eddy Curry, Antonio Davis, and a 1st round pick to New York, and received Jermaine Jackson, Mike Sweetney, Tim Thomas, two 1st round picks, and two 2nd round picks in the blockbuster.

CHAPTER 7:

DRAFT DAY

QUIZ TIME!

1. Which prospect did the Knicks select with their first-ever draft choice in 1947?

    a. Center Andy Duncan
    b. Point guard Dick McGuire
    c. Center Dick Holub
    d. Center Walter Dukes

2. The Knicks have never held the 1st overall pick in the NBA Draft in the entire history of the franchise.

    a. True
    b. False

3. How high did New York select power forward / center Kristaps Porzingis in the 2015 NBA Entry Draft?

    a. 1st round, 4th overall
    b. 2nd round, 43rd overall
    c. 2nd round, 61st overall
    d. 7th round, 222nd overall

4. Which point guard did the Knicks select highest in the NBA Entry Draft, using a 4ᵗʰ overall pick to add the floor general to their team?

   a. Dick McGuire
   b. Michael Ray Richardson
   c. Walt Frazier
   d. Mark Jackson

5. Who was the first-ever player selected by the Knicks in the NBA Entry Draft to be their lone selection for a single year?

   a. Guard Greg Anthony in 1991
   b. Swingman Trevor Ariza in 2004
   c. Guard Brian Quinnet in 1989
   d. Center Patrick Ewing in 1985

6. Which player, drafted by the Knicks, went on to score the most NBA points for another team after leaving New York?

   a. Center Bill Cartwright
   b. Center Patrick Ewing
   c. Guard Rod Strickland
   d. Center Dolph Schayes

7. New York has drafted precisely two players who have played a single game in the NBA. Their most recent, Slavko Vranes, was held off the scoresheet, but the other, Don Anielak, managed three points in his game.

   a. True
   b. False

8. The Knicks have looked to Europe for talent frequently in the NBA Entry Draft and even got as close as drafting the older brother of a future European NBA superstar at one point. Which player (unfortunately less talented than his brother) did New York select?

   a. Silvio Kukoc
   b. Thanasis Antetokounmpo
   c. Dieter Nowitzki
   d. Hernan Doncic

9. Fan favorite Sly Williams was selected, as which pick, in the 1st round by the New York Knicks in 1979?

   a. 1st
   b. 2nd
   c. 3rd
   d. 6th

10. Who was the first player ever drafted by the Knicks that did not play for an American college team?

   a. Center Nene Hilario
   b. Swingman Danilo Gallinari
   c. Center Kristaps Porzingis
   d. Center Frederic Weiss

11. When the NBA merged with the ABA in 1976 and two teams (the Kentucky Colonels and the Spirits of St. Louis) were disbanded, who did the Knicks select in the resulting dispersal draft?

   a. Center Randy Denton of the Spirits of St. Louis
   b. Guard Louie Dampier of the Kentucky Colonels

c. Center Moses Malone of the Spirits of St. Louis

d. Center Artis Gilmore of the Kentucky Colonels

12. Three times during the 2000s, New York has traded away all of its draft picks or selected players on draft day.

a. True

b. False

13. The Knicks struck out mightily in the 1950 NBA Draft, selecting nine players who scored a total of how many points in the NBA?

a. 0

b. 115

c. 307

d. 889

14. Of the draft spots in the top 10 in the NBA Draft, which spot has New York selected at more than any other?

a. 1st overall

b. 3rd overall

c. 7th overall

d. 8th overall

15. Superstar center Patrick Ewing was drafted by New York 1st overall in the 1985 NBA Entry Draft. Which of the following fellow Basketball Hall of Fame players was selected in the 4th round of that same draft?

a. Joe Dumars of the Detroit Pistons

b. Karl Malone of the Utah Jazz

c. Arvydas Sabonis of the Atlanta Hawks

d. Chris Mullin of the Golden State Warriors

16. Kristaps Porzingis was such a talented athlete coming out of college that he was drafted in not one but three sports (basketball, baseball, and football).

    a. True

    b. False

17. Up to and including the 2020 NBA Entry Draft, how many player selections have the New York Knicks made in their history?

    a. 496

    b. 602

    c. 833

    d. 1,009

18. How many times in history has New York used a top 10 overall draft pick?

    a. 26

    b. 47

    c. 60

    d. 71

19. What is the lowest position in the draft that the Knicks have selected a player who would go on to make the Naismith Memorial Basketball Hall of Fame?

    a. 6th overall

    b. 12th overall

    c. 17th overall

    d. 48th overall

20. There have been 26 players in the NBA who measured 7'3" or taller. The Knicks have never drafted any of them.

   a. True
   b. False

QUIZ ANSWERS

1. C – Center Dick Holub

2. B – False

3. A – 1st round, 4th overall

4. B – Michael Ray Richardson

5. C – Guard Brian Quinnet in 1989

6. D – Center Dolph Schayes

7. A – True

8. B – Thanasis Antetokounmpo

9. C – 3rd

10. D – Center Frederic Weiss

11. A – Center Randy Denton of the Spirits of St. Louis

12. B – False

13. B – 115

14. D – 8th overall

15. C – Arvydas Sabonis of the Atlanta Hawks

16. B – False

17. A – 496

18. B – 47

19. C – 17th overall

20. B – False

DID YOU KNOW?

1. Between 1979 and 1983, New York enjoyed a stretch in which they selected at least one player per year who lasted at least 700 games in the NBA. During those years, they hit on, Bill Cartwright, Kurt Rambis, Mike Woodson, Frank Brickowski, Trent Tucker, and Darrell Walker.

2. Despite the major draft success of 1959 pick power forward Johnny Green, who would go on to top 1,000 NBA games played, 12,000 points scored, and 9,000 rebounds grabbed, the Knicks have only chosen one other player from Green's Michigan State Spartans since that selection. That was Peter Davis, in 1975, with no one else taken since then.

3. Of all the players drafted in New York history, point guard Mark Jackson leads the NBA in most games played (1,296) and assists (10,334).

4. Perhaps not surprisingly, New York has drafted 15 players from the St. John's Red Storm, who share Madison Square Garden with the Knicks. This is the most players the team has selected from any school, and includes stalwart point guards Dick McGuire and Mark Jackson.

5. The first Knicks draft pick who went on to record over 5,000 NBA assists was guard Walt Frazier, who the team chose in 1967. Frazier became a Knicks icon, although his

assists mark was later surpassed by Rod Strickland and Mark Jackson.

6. New York has held the 8th overall pick seven times, more than any other spot in the draft. They have never elected to trade that selection. When keeping it, their best draft picks from the spot have been centers Willis Reed, Channing Frye, and Jordan Hill.

7. The largest Knicks draft class ever was selected in 1960, when the team drafted a whopping 18 players over the course of the draft, including three players from the University of California. Top choice, center Darrall Imhoff (of California) worked out the best, but only two of the other selections would ever suit up in the NBA.

8. When the NBA expanded to Canada in 1995, both the Toronto Raptors and Vancouver Grizzlies participated in an expansion draft to fill their rosters. With the 2nd overall pick in that draft, Vancouver plucked point guard Greg Anthony away from the Knicks, and he toiled for the Grizzlies until 1997.

9. In the 1948 NBA Draft, New York chose two centers, Dolph Schayes and Harry Gallatin. Both Schayes and Gallatin would be elected to the Basketball Hall of Fame, although Schayes never played for the Knicks, opting to sign with the rival National Basketball League's Syracuse Nationals instead.

10. The latest pick the Knicks have made in the NBA Draft was Mike Henderson from Long Island University Post,

whom the team chose 223rd overall in 1984. Henderson never made it to the NBA. Point guard Milt Williams, the team's 202nd overall pick from Lincoln University of Missouri in 1968, was the latest pick they've made who actually played for the team.

CHAPTER 8:

THE GUARDS

QUIZ TIME!

1. Which two guards played more games than any other players for New York during the team's challenging first season in the NBA in 1946-47, suiting up for 60 games each to pace the team?

    a. Ossie Schectman and Bud Palmer
    b. Stan Stutz and Tommy Byrnes
    c. Ralph Kaplowitz and Sonny Hertzberg
    d. Bob Cluggish and Bob Fitzgerald

2. Knicks shooting guard John Starks was nearly released by the team before proving himself as a star, but an injury in practice on a dunk attempt rejected by Patrick Ewing prevented New York from being allowed to cut him, and so Starks remained with the team.

    a. True
    b. False

3. When, in 2005, the NBA decided to design a clause allowing teams to cut one player to prevent the player's

contract from being considered in luxury tax calculations, the clause was popularly referred to as what, in recognition of a Knicks player many thought it was designed for?

a. "The John Starks Amendment"
b. "The Steve Francis Exception"
c. "The Stephon Marbury Clause"
d. "The Allan Houston Rule"

4. Which guard has played more minutes in the Knicks lineup than anyone else other than Patrick Ewing?

a. Richie Guerin
b. Walt Frazier
c. Allan Houston
d. Earl Monroe

5. The initials in popular Knicks guard R.J. Barrett's name actually stand for what?

a. Randall Joseph
b. Raymond James
c. Rodarius Jamal
d. Rowan Jr.

6. Which of the following is NOT true about legendary Knicks guard Earl Monroe?

a. He began his own record label in the 1980s called Pretty Pearl Records.
b. He started his own business in 2012 called the NBA Candy Store.

c. He designed his own sneaker in 1997 called Black Jesus Kicks.

d. He opened his own restaurant in 2005 called Earl Monroe's Restaurant & Pearl Club.

7. It is a Knicks tradition for every point guard to lob an alley-oop for each teammate during the warm-up before a home playoff game.

a. True
b. False

8. Which of the following is NOT a training technique practiced by dedicated Knicks guard Bill Bradley as a young basketball player?

a. Practicing 3.5 hours every weekday and eight hours on Saturdays

b. Adding 10 pounds of lead to his shoes to increase his leg strength

c. Wearing glasses with cardboard blocking his vision of the floor so he learned to dribble without looking down

d. Shooting at a garbage can with a 12-inch diameter instead of a regulation 18-inch rim to hone his accuracy

9. Which Knicks point guard holds the franchise record for most assists recorded in a single game, with 22 passes converted into points?

a. Mark Jackson
b. John Starks

c. Chris Duhon

d. Walt Frazier

10. Point guard Chris Childs recorded his first Knicks triple-double against which NBA team on January 24, 1997?

a. New Jersey Nets

b. Charlotte Hornets

c. Golden State Warriors

d. Orlando Magic

11. Knicks mainstay Carl Braun played over 700 NBA games with the club, one of six players to do so, making him rank where overall for games played for New York?

a. 1st overall

b. Tied for 3rd overall

c. 4th overall

d. 6th overall

12. Years after his playing career was over, New York point guard Richie Guerin became a stockbroker, and landed a position as managing director with Bear, Stearns, and Co.,one of the largest global investment banks on Wall Street.

a. True

b. False

13. While playing for New York, Knicks guard Latrell Sprewell was the first NBA player to ever accomplish which of the following feats?

a. Score over 25 points in a single game, using only slam dunks
b. Create 10 steals and commit 10 turnovers in the same game
c. Shoot 0 for 10 from the free throw line during a single game
d. Shoot nine for nine in three-point shots during a single game

14. Which of these current Knicks guards has been with the team for four seasons, the longest current tenure in New York's backcourt?

    a. Dennis Smith Jr.
    b. Austin Rivers
    c. Frank Ntilikina
    d. Immanuel Quickley

15. Which of the following 50-point facts about Knicks guard Jamal Crawford is NOT true?

    a. Crawford's 51 points in a game is the highest total ever scored by a player coming off the bench.
    b. Crawford is the only NBA player ever to score 50 points with four different franchises.
    c. Crawford is the oldest NBA player ever to score 50 points in a game.
    d. Crawford is in the top 10 NBA players of all time in most 50-point games.

16. Former Knicks point guard Walt Frazier was the first guard in NBA history to hit a three-pointer after the

institution of the three-point line was approved in 1979 following years of debate.

a. True
b. False

17. Which of the following achievements has Knicks guard Bill Bradley NOT accomplished in his post NBA playing career?

a. Hosted his own talk show on Sirius Satellite Radio
b. Run for president of the United States of America
c. Purchased a horse named Long Shot, which won the Kentucky Derby
d. Become a corporate director of Starbucks

18. One New York point guard served in the United States Marine Corps for several years. Who was this brave player?

a. Richie Guerin
b. Dick McGuire
c. Paul Westphal
d. Charlie Ward

19. Which New York Knicks guard once punched Los Angeles Lakers superstar Kobe Bryant in the throat during a game?

a. John Starks
b. Chris Childs
c. Doug Christie
d. Latrell Sprewell

20. Knicks guard John Starks set an interesting record by recording 39 consecutive assists to the same player (teammate Patrick Ewing).

    a. True
    b. False

QUIZ ANSWERS

1. B – Stan Stutz and Tommy Byrnes

2. A – True

3. D – "The Allan Houston Rule"

4. B – Walt Frazier

5. D – Rowan Jr.

6. C – He designed his own sneaker in 1997 called Black Jesus Kicks.

7. B – False

8. D – Shooting at a garbage can with a 12-inch diameter instead of a regulation 18-inch rim to hone his accuracy

9. C – Chris Duhon

10. B – Charlotte Hornets

11. C – 4th overall

12. A – True

13. D – Shoot nine for nine in three-point shots during a single game

14. C – Frank Ntilikina

15. D – Crawford is in the top 10 NBA players of all time in most 50-point games.

16. B – False

17. C – Purchased a horse named Long Shot, which won the Kentucky Derby

18. A – Richie Guerin

19. B – Chris Childs

20. B – False

DID YOU KNOW?

1. Only two NBA players have ever taken home an Olympic gold medal, an NBA championship, and a EuroLeague title. For almost four decades, Knicks guard Bill Bradley was the only one, until he was joined in 2004 by San Antonio Spurs guard Manu Ginobili.

2. New York icon Walt Frazier wasn't done with the Knicks after retiring from his playing career in 1979. Frazier became a broadcaster, and to this day, he does color commentary for Knicks contests on the MSG network.

3. Known nearly as much for his sense of style as his playing ability or broadcasting skills, Walt Frazier was honored with a website created explicitly to track and rate his attire in the Knicks' broadcast booth. Using Frazier's nickname, the site creators dubbed their web page ClydeSoFly.com.

4. Knicks swingman Bill Bradley was successful on the court for New York, but became even more successful off of it. Bradley became a United States Senator for the Democratic Party and served three terms in Congress.

5. During the prime years of his career, Knicks shooting guard Carl Braun missed two full seasons with the team because of his military commitments. Braun is credited as the originator of the popular term "swish," which he

developed to describe the sound a good shot made as it passed through the net.

6. New York guard Jamal Crawford has made more four-point plays (hitting a three-pointer and then converting a free throw afterward) than any other player in NBA history.

7. Nine point guards who have played for the Knicks have been enshrined in the Basketball Hall of Fame. Four were honored very recently, with Maurice Cheeks and Jason Kidd getting the nod in 2018, and Carl Braun and Paul Westphal inducted in 2019.

8. Popular Knicks shooting guard Allan Houston became a successful executive after his playing career ended. Houston is a special assistant to New York's general manager, and is himself the general manager of the Westchester Knicks, New York's G League team.

9. Knicks point guard Jeremy Lin was the first NBA player born of Taiwanese descent. His background sparked massive increases in the popularity of basketball in both Taiwan and China, and Lin became the only Asian-American to capture an NBA title in 2019.

10. Every year on his wedding anniversary, former Knicks guard Doug Christie and his wife Jackie celebrate by getting remarried. They throw a reception complete with family members, invited guests, and even a wedding cake.

CHAPTER 9:

CENTERS OF ATTENTION

QUIZ TIME!

1. Champion Knicks center Willis Reed was raised on a farm in which female named city?

   a. Charlotte, North Carolina

   b. Alexandria, Virginia

   c. Helena, Montana

   d. Bernice, Louisiana

2. Knicks center Bill Cartwright, who played eight years with the team, was born and raised in Brooklyn, New York.

   a. True

   b. False

3. Only one center has played an entire career of at least 10 years for the Knicks without ever starting a game for another NBA franchise. Which loyal center played only for New York?

   a. Walt Bellamy

   b. Patrick Ewing

c. Willis Reed

d. Bob McAdoo

4. Which Knicks center served mainly as Patrick Ewing's substitute during his time with the Knicks, starting just 29 of nearly 300 New York games during his tenure?

a. Frederic Weiss

b. Arvydas Sabonis

c. Jeffrey Neill

d. Eddie Lee Wilkins

5. Big man Patrick Ewing suffered a devastating injury in 1997 when he landed on his hand after falling on the court, which of the following issues was Ewing NOT diagnosed with as a result of his hard landing?

a. A dislocated lunate bone

b. A displaced fracture

c. Torn ligaments

d. Nerve damage

6. Knicks center Bill Cartwright coached globally after retiring from his playing career, and led teams in all of the following countries except which one?

a. United States of America

b. Japan

c. Greece

d. Mexico

7. Knicks center Patrick Ewing, 7'0," once had a shot blocked by 5'3" Charlotte Hornets point guard Muggsy Bogues.

a. True

b. False

8. Knicks franchise center Patrick Ewing was born in which country on August 5, 1962?

a. United States of America

b. Democratic Republic of Congo

c. Jamaica

d. Argentina

9. Although talented center Amar'e Stoudemire was unable to lead the New York Knicks to a championship, he did win titles with two different teams in which league after his NBA career ended?

a. Israeli Basketball Premier League

b. Lega Basket Serie A (Italy)

c. Novo Basquete Brasil

d. Basketball Bundesliga (Germany)

10. Center Willis Reed played his entire NBA career, lasting how many years, with the New York Knicks after they selected him 8th overall in 1964?

a. 14 seasons

b. 8 seasons

c. 16 seasons

d. 10 seasons

11. Which center has recorded the most career turnovers while with the New York Knicks?

a. Bill Cartwright

b. Patrick Ewing

c. Marcus Camby

d. Amar'e Stoudemire

12. Future New York pivot Walt Bellamy led the NBA in field goal percentage in his rookie season in the league.

a. True

b. False

13. In the 2019-20 NBA season, Knicks center Mitchell Robinson shot 74.2% on his field goals, breaking a longstanding NBA record held by which superstar center?

a. Kareem Abdul-Jabbar of the Los Angeles Lakers

b. Wilt Chamberlain of the Philadelphia 76ers

c. Hakeem Olajuwon of the Houston Rockets

d. Bill Russell of the Boston Celtics

14. Which Knicks reserve center was forced to come off the bench and guard superstar Wilt Chamberlain against the Los Angeles Lakers in the 1970 NBA Finals when starting center Willis Reed was hurt?

a. Nate Bowman

b. Greg Fillmore

c. Jerry Lucas

d. Dave Stallworth

15. Which of the following facts about decorated Knicks center Buck Williams is NOT true?

a. His real name is Charles Linwood Williams.

b. He is one of seven players to reach 16,000 points and 13,000 rebounds in a career.

c. He was selected to the United States' Olympic basketball team, but never played for them due to America's boycott of the 1980 games in Moscow.

d. He was an All-Star three times in his career, with two of those appearances coming as a member of the Knicks.

16. No Knicks center has ever led the team in points scored during a single game.

   a. True

   b. False

17. How did Knicks center Amar'e Stoudemire injure his hand during the 2011-12 NBA playoffs?

   a. He dislocated a finger while attempting to block a shot against Heat center Alonzo Mourning.

   b. He broke it during a dive for a loose ball when teammate Tyson Chandler stepped on it accidentally.

   c. He cut his hand on a fire extinguisher that he had angrily punched after the team lost a game.

   d. He lost a fingernail when a rough edge caught on his jersey and tore off as he was dressing for a game.

18. During the famous Game 7 matchup of the 1970 NBA Finals, which would come to be known as "The Willis Reed Game," injured center Willis Reed limped onto the court with the Knicks facing the Los Angeles Lakers and inspired his team to a victory that exemplified his clutch competitiveness. How many points did Reed score in that game?

a. 4

b. 19

c. 28

d. 41

19. Which of the following achievements has New York center Patrick Ewing NOT accomplished twice?

   a. Leading the Knicks to the NBA Finals

   b. Winning an Olympic gold medal

   c. Leading the NBA in blocked shots

   d. Being elected to the Basketball Hall of Fame

20. New York has had a greater number of starting players at the center spot than any other position.

   a. True

   b. False

QUIZ ANSWERS

1. D – Bernice, Louisiana

2. B – False

3. C – Willis Reed

4. D – Eddie Lee Wilkins

5. D – Nerve damage

6. C – Greece

7. A – True

8. C – Jamaica

9. A – Israeli Basketball Premier League

10. D – 10 seasons

11. B – Patrick Ewing

12. A – True

13. B – Wilt Chamberlain of the Philadelphia 76ers

14. D – Dave Stallworth

15. D – He was an All-Star three times in his career, with two of those appearances coming as a member of the Knicks.

16. B – False

17. C – He cut his hand on a fire extinguisher that he had angrily punched after the team lost a game.

18. A – 4

19. C – Leading the NBA in blocked shots

20. B – False

DID YOU KNOW?

1. Knicks center Patrick Ewing was considered such a franchise-changing player that the NBA changed its long-held draft rules the year Ewing was eligible to be selected. Rather than the bottom team in each conference flipping a coin for the right to select first, all non-playoff teams were placed in an equally weighted lottery, which is how the Knicks were able to obtain Ewing.

2. The NBA record for most games played in a single regular season is 88, held by Knicks big man Walt Bellamy. Although the season is just 82 games long, Bellamy suited up for 35 games with New York in 1968-69 before being traded to the Detroit Pistons, who had 53 games remaining, all of which Bellamy played in.

3. New York center Dikembe Mutombo was famous for two things: blocking shots and taunting opponents after the block by wagging his finger as if to say "no." Referees would sometimes call a technical foul on him, so Mutombo began wagging his finger at Knicks fans rather than members of the other team.

4. Before the Knicks took center Mitchell Robinson in the 2018 NBA Draft, he had spent the year previous training by himself. Robinson's approach was unique; he was the first-ever player chosen in a draft who had not played for any team (high school, college, or professional) in the year preceding his selection.

5. The Knicks' Buck Williams was a tough center who excelled at rebounding, but his lasting claim to fame remains the protective goggles he wore on the court throughout most of his career. Williams sported the goggles after taking an elbow to the eye as a young player.

6. New York center Herb Williams spent the period between 1992 and 1999 with the Knicks, except for one single game as a member of the Toronto Raptors in 1996 that broke up the stretch.

7. Knicks center Amar'e Stoudemire explored a diverse array of business interests during and after his time playing for New York. Among other things, Stoudemire has acted in several television shows and movies, developed his own record label, created his own clothing line, written children's books, and started a wine label.

8. Knicks legend Patrick Ewing had an ongoing rivalry with Houston Rockets center Hakeem Olajuwon, and both would reach the pinnacle of their success against the other, one decade apart. In 1984, Ewing led his college team, the Georgetown Hoyas, to an NCAA Championship over Olajuwon's Houston Cougars squad. But in 1994, Olajuwon returned the favor, defeating Ewing and the Knicks in seven games in the NBA Finals.

9. Former Knicks center Herb Williams went on to become an assistant coach with both the New York Knicks and the New York Liberty of the Women's National Basketball Association.

10. Journeyman center Eddie Lee Wilkins served three different stints with the Knicks, in 1984-85, 1987, and 1988-91. During the gaps in between those tenures, Wilkins played for eight different teams, none of which were in the NBA.

CHAPTER 10:

THE FORWARDS

QUIZ TIME!

1. Which three languages can multi-talented Knicks forward Kristaps Porzingis speak fluently?

   a. English, Russian, and French
   b. English, German, and Italian
   c. English, Spanish, and Latvian
   d. Russian, German, and Chinese

2. Ernie Vandeweghe and his son Kiki Vandeweghe both played forward in the NBA, and both began their tenure with the New York Knicks exactly 40 years apart; Ernie in 1949 and Kiki in 1989.

   a. True
   b. False

3. Which type of business did Knicks enforcer and power forward Charles Oakley NOT invest in following his playing career?

a. A blues-themed night club down the street from Madison Square Garden in New York

b. Hair and nail salons run by his sisters in Cleveland

c. A steakhouse chain with restaurants in Ohio and Florida

d. A series of carwashes, some of which also include oil changes and laundromats

4. Only 13 athletes have competed professionally in both the NBA and Major League Baseball. Knicks forward Dave DeBusschere was one, as he served as a pitcher and even recorded a shutout for which MLB team before giving up baseball to focus on basketball instead?

a. Chicago White Sox

b. New York Yankees

c. Pittsburgh Pirates

d. Cleveland Indians

5. Which tough Knicks forward tied for the NBA lead in most personal fouls, with a bruising 330 during the 1974-75 season?

a. Mel Davis

b. Bill Bradley

c. Phil Jackson

d. Harthorne Wingo

6. Knicks forward David Lee got married to which famous female tennis player in 2019?

a. Anna Kournikova

b. Caroline Wozniacki

c. Venus Williams

d. Maria Sharapova

7. New York forward Ernie Vandeweghe went on to become chairman of the President's Council on Physical Fitness and Sports, as well as becoming a member of the Olympic Sports commission, during Gerald Ford's presidency in the 1970s.

a. True

b. False

8. What did physical Knicks forward Xavier McDaniel do throughout his career in an effort to intimidate opposing players?

a. Wear a set of brass knuckles on each hand to the games, noticeably taking them off just before the start

b. Growl like a pit bull whenever he went up for a rebound

c. Shave his head completely, including his eyebrows

d. Walk to center court before tip-off and flex his considerable biceps towards whoever he was guarding that night

9. The Knicks' team record for most consecutive games with at least 20 points scored belongs to which forward, who set the mark at 31 straight contests?

a. Bernard King

b. Spencer Haywood

c. Charles Oakley

d. Carmelo Anthony

10. No less an authority than NBA MVP Kevin Durant was impressed with the unique skills of Knicks rookie forward Kristaps Porzingis in 2015, which resulted in Durant calling Porzingis which of the following?

   a. "A magician on the court"
   b. "The 8th wonder of the world"
   c. "A basketball unicorn"
   d. "The next me"

11. Which of the following is NOT true about New York Knicks small forward Kiki Vandeweghe?

   a. He contributed 51 points against the Detroit Pistons in the highest scoring NBA game of all time.
   b. His mother was a former Miss America pageant winner.
   c. He married Elisabeth Riley, the daughter of his coach in New York, Pat Riley.
   d. He was booed every time the Knicks played in Dallas, as Vandeweghe had declined to play for the Mavericks after they drafted him.

12. Undrafted forward Lance Thomas signed multiple 10-day contracts with the New York Knicks during which his NBA career hung in the balance. Thomas persevered and thrived until he was eventually named co-captain of the team.

   a. True
   b. False

13. Which of the following is NOT a movie or television show in which Knicks small forward Carmelo Anthony has guest starred?

    a. *Sons of Anarchy*
    b. *Teenage Mutant Ninja Turtles*
    c. *Nurse Jackie*
    d. *Harry Potter and the Order of the Phoenix*

14. New York forward Ken Sears notched a notable accomplishment on December 20, 1954, when he became the earliest basketball player to appear on the cover of which popular magazine?

    a. *Reader's Digest*
    b. *Time*
    c. *Sports Illustrated*
    d. *Rolling Stone*

15. Which of the following geographical facts about forward Carmelo Anthony is NOT true?

    a. He was born in Brooklyn, New York.
    b. He went to high school in Buffalo, New York.
    c. He went to college in Syracuse, New York.
    d. He played basketball for the Knicks, in New York.

16. After engaging in two memorable fights with his former Chicago teammates as a newly traded member of the New York Knicks, ex-Bull Charles Oakley earned the nickname "The Bullfighter" in the press.

    a. True
    b. False

17. Which former New York Knicks forward often fills in for former Knicks guard Walt Frazier doing color commentary on MSG broadcasts when Frazier has to miss a game?

   a. Charles Oakley
   b. David Lee
   c. Bernard King
   d. Allan Houston

18. Only three NBA players have scored more than 10,000 points with multiple NBA franchises. Forward Carmelo Anthony accomplished this with the Knicks and which other team?

   a. Oklahoma City Thunder
   b. Portland Trail Blazers
   c. Houston Rockets
   d. Denver Nuggets

19. Counting both regular season and playoffs, one Knicks forward started a team-record 107 games during a single season. Which forward notched this ironman mark?

   a. Willie Naulls
   b. Charles Oakley
   c. Carmelo Anthony
   d. Anthony Mason

20. When the career of Knicks forward Michael Sweetney did not take off as he had hoped, Sweetney left the NBA and spent a decade playing in other professional leagues, including seasons for teams in Uruguay, Puerto Rico, and Venezuela.

a. True
b. False

QUIZ ANSWERS

1. C – English, Spanish, and Latvian

2. A – True

3. A – A blues-themed night club down the street from Madison Square Garden in New York

4. A – Chicago White Sox

5. C – Phil Jackson

6. B – Caroline Wozniacki

7. A – True

8. C – Shave his head completely, including his eyebrows

9. D – Carmelo Anthony

10. C – "A basketball unicorn"

11. C – He married Elisabeth Riley, the daughter of his coach in New York, Pat Riley.

12. A – True

13. D – *Harry Potter and the Order of the Phoenix*

14. C – *Sports Illustrated*

15. B – He went to high school in Buffalo, New York.

16. B – False

17. C – Bernard King

18. D – Denver Nuggets

19. B – Charles Oakley

20. A – True

DID YOU KNOW?

1. When the Knicks made small forward Wille Naulls captain of the team in 1960, it marked the first time a team in any popular American sport had given the title to an African-American player. Naulls lived up to the pressure, setting a New York record for points that same year and making the All-Star Team.

2. Knicks forward Jared Jeffries chose a unique path in his post-playing career. Jeffries combined his outgoing personality with his love of fishing to host a television show that featured him going after fish in various locations. *Modern Fishing With Jared Jeffries* was a success and lasted four seasons on the Outdoor Channel.

3. Well after his playing days with the Knicks were in the past, former Knicks forward Charles Oakley has had an ongoing feud with New York owner James Dolan. The two have criticized each other in the press, and Oakley was even arrested after refusing to leave Madison Square Garden when Dolan had security guards attempt to throw him out in 2017.

4. In the 22 years between 1998 and 2019, the Knicks have rostered a forward with the surname Thomas for 16 of them. Kurt Thomas played for the team from 1998 to 2005, overlapping with Tim Thomas for the last two years of that period. Tim Thomas returned in 2008-09, followed by

Kurt Thomas's return in 2012-13. The next year, Lance Thomas took over and remained in New York from 2014 to 2019.

5. The Vandeweghe family was chock-full of successful athletes. Not only did father and son, Ernie and Kiki, both play forward for the Knicks, but Ernie's other children (Kiki's siblings) had great talent as well. Tauna Vandeweghe became an Olympic swimmer, Heather Vandeweghe captained the American women's national polo team, and Bruk Vandeweghe earned a Goodwill Games medal in beach volleyball.

6. During the first game of the first playoff series of forward Tim Thomas's first season with the New York Knicks, Thomas was fouled hard by Jason Collins of the New Jersey Nets and left the court on a stretcher. Thomas would miss the rest of the playoffs with his injury.

7. Knicks forward Charles Smith was popular with his peers and spent his post-playing career thinking of other players. Smith took part in founding a non-profit organization designed to help struggling retired players, then became executive director of the National Basketball Retired Players Association where he staged many exhibition games for former players.

8. Popular Knicks forward Malik Rose played for four NBA teams during his playing career and worked for four NBA organizations after he had retired. The Knicks are the only team that fits into both categories, as Rose spent a season

as a pregame analyst in New York immediately after retiring.

9. In the 1970s, the New York Knicks featured a lineup with three Hall of Fame forwards. Phil Jackson, Bill Bradley, and Spencer Haywood all suited up together. A fourth Hall-of-Famer, Bob McAdoo, played both power forward and center. And the icing on the cake was that the Knicks also had two Hall of Fame guards, Earl Monroe and Walt Frazier.

10. Knicks forward Carmelo Anthony has starred in four Olympic Summer Games for Team USA, where his teams have taken home three gold medals and one bronze medal. Anthony is the all-time leader for Team USA in most Olympic games played (31), points scored (336), and rebounds grabbed (125).

CHAPTER 11:

COACHES, GMS, & OWNERS

QUIZ TIME!

1. Who served as the Knicks' first general manager?

    a. Eddie Donovan

    b. Ned Irish

    c. Fred Podesta

    d. Vince Boryla

2. When the NBA celebrated its 50th anniversary in 1996, it named the top 10 coaches in league history, and included three Knicks coaches, Red Holzman, Don Nelson, and Pat Riley.

    a. True

    b. False

3. The Knicks' first head coach, Neil Cohalan, lasted for how long in that position with the franchise?

    a. 12 games

    b. 1 season

    c. 9 seasons

    d. 16 seasons

4. The Knicks' most recent coach, Tom Thibodeau, rose through the coaching ranks as an assistant at which NCAA program?

   a. Duke University
   b. University of North Carolina
   c. Harvard University
   d. University of Nevada Las Vegas

5. Who has owned the New York Knicks for the longest amount of time?

   a. Ned Irish
   b. Cablevision
   c. James Dolan
   d. Gulf and Western

6. Of all the New York bench bosses who have coached over 100 NBA games with the team, which one had the lowest winning percentage at only .202?

   a. Derek Fisher
   b. Eddie Donovan
   c. Isiah Thomas
   d. David Fizdale

7. New York is the only NBA franchise to have a player rise from playing for the team to ownership of the team.

   a. True
   b. False

8. Which coach led the Knicks to their first NBA championship?

a. Joe Lapchick

b. Eddie Donovan

c. Red Holzman

d. Rick Pitino

9. Which of the following New York executives did NOT take the floor as a player on the team before getting the chance to guide it from the front office?

a. Phil Jackson

b. Dave DeBusschere

c. Vince Boryla

d. Dave Checketts

10. Who is the New York leader in all-time coaching wins with the franchise?

a. Red Holzman

b. Jeff Van Gundy

c. Hubey Brown

d. Pat Riley

11. Future Knicks leader Isiah Thomas was actually a Hall of Fame NBA player who spent his entire career with which other franchise?

a. New Jersey Nets

b. Chicago Bulls

c. Golden State Warriors

d. Detroit Pistons

12. Current New York Knicks owner James Dolan moonlights as a blues singer in a band called JD & The Straight Shot,

which has released several studio albums and performed at gigs with notable bands like The Dixie Chicks, ZZ Top, and the Eagles.

a. True

b. False

13. How many of the Knicks' 31 head coaches have spent their entire NBA coaching career with New York?

a. 2

b. 5

c. 8

d. 15

14. Which Knicks head coach has led the franchise to the most playoff appearances?

a. Jeff Van Gundy

b. Pat Riley

c. Joe Lapchick

d. Red Holzman

15. Out of 14 seasons coaching the Knicks, how many times did coach Red Holzman finish above .500?

a. 3

b. 8

c. 10

d. 14

16. At one point in their history, the Knicks employed four coaches over a decade who had all started for New York at some point during their playing careers.

a. True

b. False

17. How did James Dolan become the majority owner of the New York Knicks in 2010?

a. He purchased the team when the previous owners wished to sell.

b. He inherited the team from his father.

c. He forced a takeover of the corporation that had previously owned the team.

d. He became CEO of Cablevision, the company that owned the team.

18. Knicks general manager Glen Grunwald was once the Director of Athletics for which post-secondary school in Ontario, Canada?

a. University of Toronto

b. Brock University

c. McMaster University

d. University of Waterloo

19. Two Knicks coaches have won the NBA Coach of the Year Award while behind the bench for New York. Which two coaches accomplished this feat while finishing with identical 60-22 records during their best seasons?

a. Red Holzman and Pat Riley

b. Dick McGwire and Don Nelson

c. Hubey Brown and Jeff Van Gundy

d. Lenny Wilkens and Mike D'Antoni

20. Knicks owner James Dolan once proposed trading franchises with New York Yankees owner George Steinbrenner, as part of a business deal.

    a. True
    b. False

QUIZ ANSWERS

1. B – Ned Irish

2. A – True

3. B – 1 season

4. C – Harvard University

5. A – Ned Irish

6. D – David Fizdale

7. B – False

8. C – Red Holzman

9. D – Dave Checketts

10. A – Red Holzman

11. D – Detroit Pistons

12. A – True

13. C – 8

14. D – Red Holzman

15. B – 8

16. B – False

17. D – He became CEO of Cablevision, the company that owned the team.

18. C – McMaster University

19. A – Red Holzman and Pat Riley

20. B – False

DID YOU KNOW?

1. Ned Irish, who served as the Knicks' very first general manager, took the position after earlier career stops as a journalist who covered sports and as the leader of the information bureau of the National Football League.

2. Four men have served as both coach and general manager of the Knicks. Vince Boryla coached the team for two years between 1956 and 1958 and then handled the personnel duties during 1960-61. Eddie Donovan coached from 1961 to 1965 and then stepped directly into the GM office. Red Holzman and Isiah Thomas both attempted to do both jobs at once, overlapping in each of their tenures with New York.

3. Knicks forward and (later) general manager Phil Jackson has authored eight books, including *Take It All*; a personal account of New York's NBA championship in 1970. Despite over a dozen years spent with the Knicks, Jackson is more famous for his time spent coaching superstars such as Michael Jordan, Shaquille O'Neal, and Kobe Bryant.

4. Knicks star Dave DeBusschere not only had a standout playing career with New York and became director of the team's basketball operations afterward; in between, DeBusschere served as the commissioner of the rival American Basketball Association and was a key part in the merger between that league and the NBA in 1976.

5. Phil Jackson was not the only one to write a book about the Knicks' championship season in 1969-70. Fellow teammate and later Knicks executive Dave DeBusschere composed his own take on that year, entitled *The Open Man*.

6. Knicks President Dave Checketts was the orchestrator of New York's most recent successful period. He remained in the position for just four seasons, but the Knicks twice made the playoffs, progressed to the NBA Finals, and established new high water marks in TV ratings, attendance, and revenue while Checketts was at the helm.

7. Glen Grunwald and Isiah Thomas made a powerful executive team. In 2006, Grunwald became the Knicks' vice president of basketball operations, while Thomas was the team's head coach. The duo had partnered up previously with the Toronto Raptors, where Thomas served as general manager with Grunwald as his assistant.

8. Knicks general manager Steve Mills was born in New York and grew up as a Knicks fan, but entered the business world after graduating from Princeton University. He was lured away from his company by the NBA, and later went on to supervise the New York Knicks, Rangers, and Liberty before focusing specifically on the Knicks.

9. In an awkward arrangement, Isiah Thomas was retained as a consultant to the team after he was fired as the Knicks' president of basketball operations. However, he was forbidden from speaking with any of the team's

players as it was feared that he might not agree with the coach's message.

10. Vince "Moose" Boryla nailed the New York Knicks trifecta, serving in positions with the club as a player, head coach, and general manager. Boryla would later win the NBA's Executive of the Year Award as the GM of the Denver Nuggets.

CHAPTER 12:

THE AWARDS SECTION

QUIZ TIME!

1. Which Knick has won the most Maurice Podoloff Trophies as league MVP while playing for New York?

   a. Guard Walt Frazier

   b. Center Willis Reed

   c. Center Patrick Ewing

   d. Forward Carmelo Anthony

2. The first Knick to win any major award given out by the NBA was forward Dave DeBusschere.

   a. True

   b. False

3. During which season did the Knicks win their first Larry O'Brien Trophy as NBA champions?

   a. 1948-49

   b. 1957-58

   c. 1969-70

   d. 1972-73

4. In 1996, the NBA announced its 50 Greatest Players in NBA history. How many of these players suited up for the Knicks?

    a. 0
    b. 1
    c. 2
    d. 6

5. The J. Walter Kennedy Trophy, given out to an NBA player who shows "great service and dedication to the community," has been awarded to which Knicks?

    a. Forwards Carmelo Anthony, Phil Jackson, and David Lee
    b. Forward Bill Bradley and center Dikembe Mutombo
    c. Guards Mike Glenn and Rory Sparrow
    d. Guards Charlie Ward and James Lin

6. How many Knicks have won the Twyman-Stokes Trophy as NBA Teammate of the Year thanks to "selfless play and commitment and dedication to his team"?

    a. 0
    b. 3
    c. 9
    d. 11

7. In the team's illustrious history, no New York Knick has ever led the NBA in scoring for a single season.

    a. True
    b. False

8. Who was the most recent New York player to make the NBA All-Rookie First Team?

   a. Center Mitchell Robinson
   b. Center Willie Hernangomez
   c. Guard Tim Hardaway Jr.
   d. Guard Langston Galloway

9. Which Knicks players have taken home the NBA All-Star Game MVP Award?

   a. Forward Carmelo Anthony and center Patrick Ewing
   b. Forwards Allan Houston and Larry Johnson
   c. Guards Earl Monroe and Nate Robinson
   d. Center Willis Reed and guard Walt Frazier

10. Which of these sets of Knicks includes the players who have gone on to finish a season as the league's leading scorer while with New York?

    a. Forwards Bernard King and Carmelo Anthony
    b. Center Patrick Ewing and guard Steve Francis
    c. Forward Carmelo Anthony and guard Earl Monroe
    d. Centers Patrick Ewing, Willis Reed, and Harry Gallatin

11. The Sixth Man of the Year Award for best performing player as a substitute has been won by which three Knicks in franchise history?

    a. Forward Charles Smith, center Buck Williams, and guard John Starks
    b. Center Buck Williams and forwards David Lee and Charles Oakley

c. Forward Anthony Mason and guards John Starks and J.R. Smith

d. Guard Nate Robinson, center Dave Stallworth, and forward Phil Jackson

12. Guard Nate Robinson is the only New York Knick to ever be crowned the NBA's Slam Dunk Contest champion, taking home the title three times during the 2000s.

a. True

b. False

13. Which of the following Knicks players did NOT win the Eddie Gottlieb Trophy as the league's top rookie?

a. Center Patrick Ewing

b. Guard Mark Jackson

c. Center Willis Reed

d. Guard Walt Frazier

14. Guard Carl Braun is first among the Knicks in the Basketball Hall of Fame starting in what year to play with the team?

a. 1946

b. 1947

c. 1953

d. 1958

15. Which Knicks player has been selected to the most NBA All-Star Games while playing for New York?

a. Center Willis Reed

b. Guard Walt Frazier

c. Forward Carmelo Anthony

d. Center Patrick Ewing

16. The New York Knicks were named the NBA's Franchise of the Century when the NBA announced the award on December 28, 1999.

a. True

b. False

17. Which New York Knick has won the most three-point shootout challenges during NBA All-Star Weekend?

a. Forward Allan Houston

b. Guard John Starks

c. Forward Carmelo Anthony

d. No Knick has ever won this event.

18. Who was the most recent New York player to make the NBA All-Defensive First Team?

a. Center Tyson Chandler in 2012-13

b. Center Mitchell Robinson in 2019-20

c. Forward Charles Oakley in 1997-98

d. Center Patrick Ewing in 1991-92

19. In how many years did New York host the NBA's annual All-Star Game?

a. 2

b. 5

c. 10

d. 13

20. For almost two decades, computer company IBM gave an award to the NBA player judged by its programming formulas to be most valuable to his team. Center Patrick Ewing received the award twice for New York.

    a. True

    b. False

QUIZ ANSWERS

1. B – Center Willis Reed

2. B – False

3. C – 1969-70

4. D – 6

5. C – Guards Mike Glenn and Rory Sparrow

6. A – 0

7. B – False

8. B – Center Willie Hernangomez

9. D – Center Willis Reed and guard Walt Frazier

10. A – Forwards Bernard King and Carmelo Anthony

11. C – Forward Anthony Mason and guards John Starks and J.R. Smith

12. B – False

13. D – Guard Walt Frazier

14. B – 1947

15. D – Center Patrick Ewing

16. B – False

17. D – No Knick has ever won this event.

18. A – Center Tyson Chandler in 2012-13

19. B – 5

20. B – False

DID YOU KNOW?

1. The Joe Dumars Trophy, for sportsmanship, ethical behavior, fair play, and integrity has been won by just one Knick in history. Point guard Jason Kidd was honored with this award in 2012-13.

2. Each year, the NBA denotes three teams' worth of All-NBA players, and the Knicks have been well represented over the years. Patrick Ewing faced stiff competition at center during his career, but still made All-NBA seven times.

3. Only four players have earned the NBA's relatively new Lifetime Achievement Award. Thus far, none of them have played for the Knicks at any point in their careers.

4. When the NBA announced its top 10 teams in history in 1996, the 1969-70 edition of the Knicks made the cut, showing they deserved respect despite the lowest winning percentage on the list.

5. For a brief period (seven years) in the early 1980s, the NBA awarded a Comeback Player of the Year trophy. In 1982-83, Knicks guard Paul Westphal snagged the award when he returned to his usual form after injuries.

6. It took until the 2011-12 season for a New York Knick to win the NBA's Defensive Player of the Year Award.

Center Tyson Chandler was the first to do so, and remains the only Knick granted the award to this day.

7. No New York Knick has ever taken home the NBA's annual Most Improved Player Award.

8. Only one Knick has ever won the Bill Russell Trophy as MVP of the NBA Finals. Center Willis Reed took home the award twice, in 1970 and 1973, during both of New York's championship runs.

9. The Knicks feature two winners of the NBA All-Star Weekend Slam Dunk Contest. Guard Nate Robinson, 5'9," used his impressive vertical leap to take home the title three times, but forward Kenny Walker was the first New York player to claim the event, doing so once in 1989.

10. In 1965, New York placed an incredible three players on the NBA's All-Rookie First Team. Willis Reed, Jim Barnes, and Howard Komives all received a selection.

CONCLUSION

There you have it, an amazing collection of Knicks trivia, information, and statistics at your fingertips! Regardless of how you fared on the quizzes, we hope that you found this book entertaining, enlightening, and educational.

Ideally, you knew many of these details, but also learned a good deal more about the history of the New York Knicks, their players, coaches, management, and some of the quirky stories surrounding the team. If you got a little peek into the colorful details that make being a fan so much more enjoyable, then mission accomplished!

The good news is the trivia doesn't have to stop there! Spread the word, challenge your fellow Knicks fans to see if they can do any better. Share some of the stories with the next generation to help them become New York supporters too.

If you are a big enough Knicks fan, consider creating your own quiz with some of the details you know that weren't presented here, and then test your friends to see if they can match your knowledge.

The New York Knicks are a storied franchise. They have a long history with multiple periods of success and a few that were less than successful. They've had glorious superstars, iconic moments, and hilarious tales, but most of all they have wonderful, passionate fans. Thank you for being one of them.